Contents

Penguins

Penguins are birds that use their wings to swim. They cannot fly. Young penguins are called chicks.

Animal Offspring

Penguins and Their Chicks

Revised Edition

Margaret Hall

Raintree is an imprint of Capstone Global Library Limited, a company incorporated in
England and Wales having its registered office at 264 Banbury Road, Oxford, OX2 7DY
– Registered company number: 6695582

www.raintree.co.uk
myorders@raintree.co.uk

ISBN 978 1 4747 5629 7 (hardback)
22 21 20 19 18
10 9 8 7 6 5 4 3 2 1

ISBN 978 1 4747 5639 6 (paperback)
23 22 21 20 19
10 9 8 7 6 5 4 3 2 1

British Library Cataloging in Publication Data
A full catalogue record for this book is available from the British Library.

Editorial Credits
Gina Kammer, editor; Sarah Bennett, designer; Morgan Walters, media researcher;
Katy LaVigne, production specialist

Printed and bound in India

Acknowledgements
We would like to thank the following for permission to reproduce photographs:
Shutterstock: Alexey Seafarer, 5, BMJ, left 21, Brandon B, 9, ChameleonsEye,
19, jo Crebbin, 7, niall dunne, 15, Roger Clark ARPS, Cover, 1, left 20, right 20,
StanislavBeloglazov, 11, vladsilver, 17, right 21, Volodymyr Goinyk, 13

Every effort has been made to contact copyright holders of material reproduced in this
book. Any omissions will be rectified in subsequent printings if notice is given to the
publisher.

All the Internet addresses (URLs) given in this book were valid at the time of going
to press. However, due to the dynamic nature of the Internet, some addresses
may have changed, or sites may have changed or ceased to exist since publication.
While the author and publisher regret any inconvenience this may cause readers,
no responsibility for any such changes can be accepted by either the author or the
publisher.

Penguins come to land

to mate and lay eggs.

Eggs

Female penguins lay one to three eggs. Some penguins keep their eggs on their feet. Other penguins keep their eggs in a nest.

Most penguin parents take turns

keeping the eggs warm.

Penguin chicks

A penguin chick hatches from the egg. Chicks have soft feathers called down.

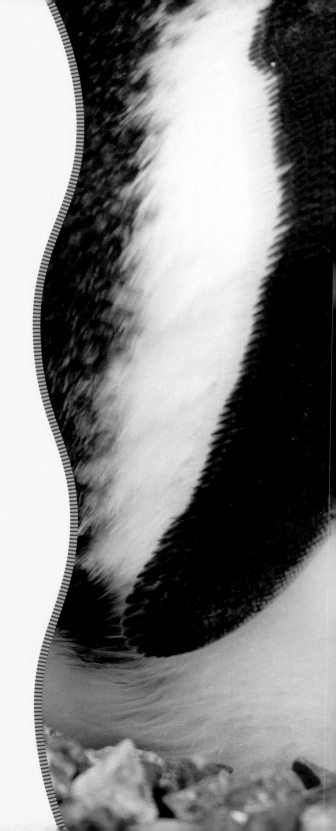

Penguin parents catch fish

for the chicks to eat.

Sometimes the chicks stand
together to keep warm.
Chicks grow new feathers
after a few months.

Growing up

Most penguins can swim and take care of themselves after about one year.

Watch penguins grow

hatching

adult after
about five years

21

Glossary

bird warm–blooded animal with wings, two legs and feathers; birds lay eggs; most birds can fly

down soft feathers of a baby bird; young penguins with down cannot swim until they grow new feathers; the new feathers are waterproof

hatch break out of an egg; a young penguin has an egg tooth on its beak; it uses the tooth to help it break the egg open

mate join together to produce young; some penguins come back to the same place every year to mate

nest place built to raise young; some penguins make nests; other penguins keep their young warm on their feet or by using their feathers

wing one of the feather–covered limbs of a bird; most birds move their wings to fly

Find out more

Books

A Penguin's Life Cycle (Watch It Grow), Charlotte Guillain (Raintree, 2012)

Shark vs Penguin (Predator vs Prey), Mary Meinking (Raintree, 2012)

Show Me Polar Animals (Show Me!), Lisa J. Amstutz (Raintree, 2017)

Websites

www.bbc.co.uk/cbeebies/watch/andys-wild-adventures-emperorpenguin
BBC

www.dkfindout.com/us/animals-and-nature/birds/penguins/
DK Find Out!

Comprehension questions

1. What does a penguin use its wings for?

2. Where can you look to find information about down feathers in this book?

3. How does standing together keep penguins warm?

Index